W9-AZO-595

OUTER SPACE
Activity Book

Freddie Levin

Dover Publications, Inc.
Mineola, New York

Copyright

Copyright © 2009 by Dover Publications, Inc.
All rights reserved.

Bibliographical Note

Outer Space Activity Book is a new work, first published by
Dover Publications, Inc., in 2009.

International Standard Book Number

ISBN-13: 978-0-486-47389-5
ISBN-10: 0-486-47389-9

Manufactured in the United States by LSC Communications

47389910   2019
www.doverpublications.com

Note

This little book is full of fun outer space activities! Here you will complete mazes, connect the dots, crossword puzzles, word searches, and more—each featuring planets, stars, rockets, astronauts, and even aliens! Try your best to complete each activity, but if you get stuck, you can turn to the solutions section, which begins on page 53. When you finish the activities, you can have even more outer space fun by coloring in the pages with crayons, colored pencils, or markers. Get ready for lift-off!

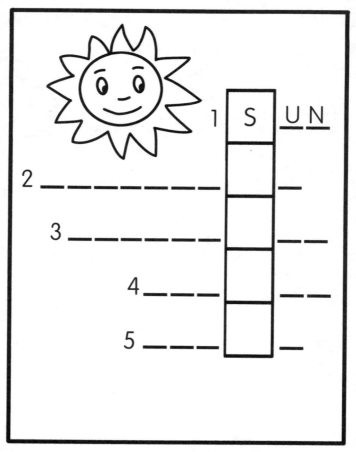

1 S | U N
2 _ _ _ _ _ _ _ _ _ _ _ | _
3 _ _ _ _ _ _ _ _ | _ _
4 _ _ _ _ | _ _
5 _ _ _ _ | _

Complete this puzzle, and you will find out what this book is all about.

Use the clues on this page to fill in the blanks in the puzzle.
Then read the word in the boxes to find the answer.

What Comes Next?

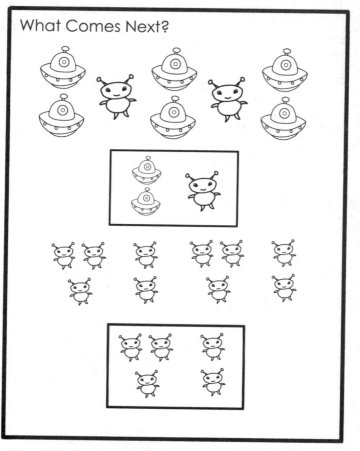

There is a pattern above each box. Circle the picture in the box that comes next in each pattern.

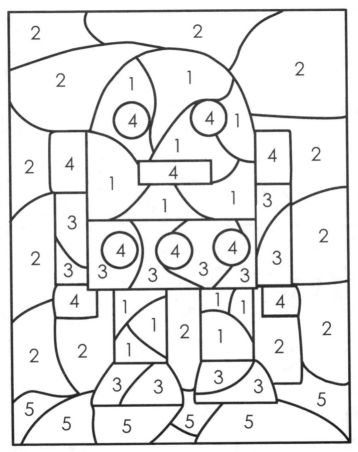

To see the picture hidden on this page, color **1** green, **2** orange,
3 blue, **4** red, and **5** black.

Look carefully at this picture of a little alien and his spaceship.

Find and circle five things that make this picture different from the one opposite.

What are some things you might see if you took a trip into space?

The numbers tell you where to write the names of the picture clues in the puzzle. One is done for you.

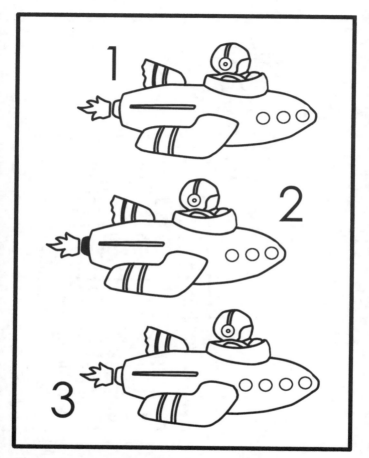

These six space pilots look the same, but only two are identical.

12

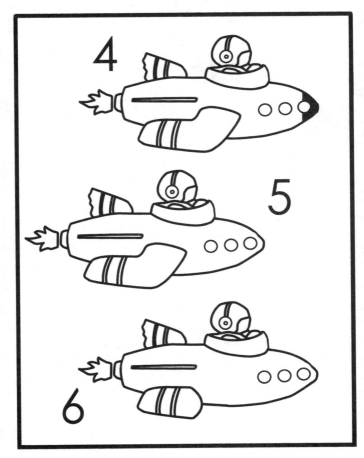

Find and circle the two that are the same.

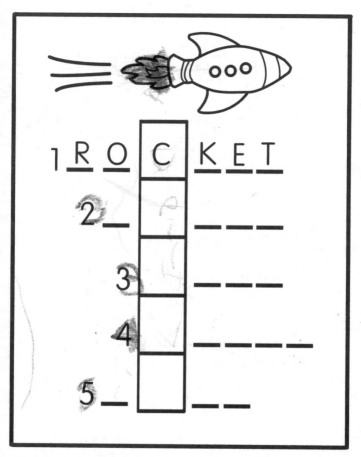

1 <u>R</u> <u>O</u> C K E T

2 _ _ _ _

3 _ _ _ _

4 _ _ _ _ _

5 _ _ _

The answer to this puzzle is something you might see streaking across the sky at night.

2

3

4

5

Use the clues on this page to fill in the blanks. Then read the word in the boxes to find out the answer.

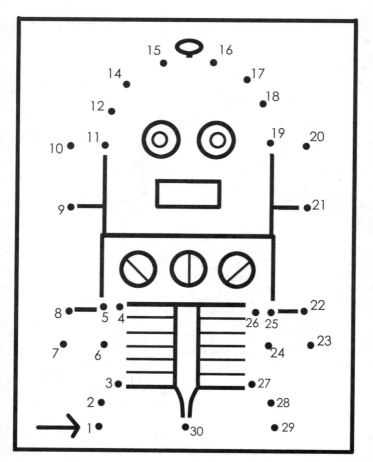

Start at the arrow and connect the dots to complete the picture.

16

If an astronaut wants to journey through space, he needs to travel in one of these. Color **R** red, **B** blue, and **Y** yellow.

Here are some more objects you can find in outer space.

18

The numbers tell you where to write the names of the picture clues in the puzzle.

Connect the dots from A to W to see one way you can travel through space. Start at the arrow.

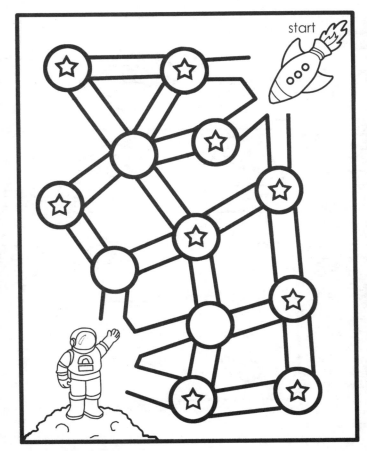

start

This rocket needs to reach the astronaut so it can take him home. Find a path through the stars without crossing any empty circles.

21

What Comes Next?

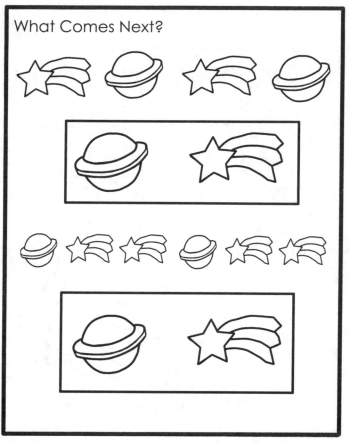

There is a pattern above each box. Circle the picture in the box that comes next in each pattern.

22

This little alien wants to go home! Start at the arrow and connect the dots to see his flying saucer.

Look carefully at this picture of a robot.

24

Find and circle seven things that make this picture different from the one opposite.

Look carefully at the picture of a space pilot.

Find and circle five things that make this picture different from the one opposite.

Count all of the flying saucers you see on these two pages.

Draw a circle around the correct number.

How do you think an alien gets around outer space? Color
□ blue, △ yellow, and ▬ red to find out.

30

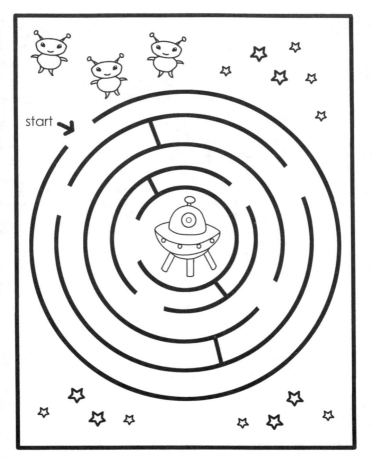

start →

Complete the maze to help these little aliens get to their spaceship.

Twinkle, twinkle little ⭐

How 👁 1der what **U R**

_____

_____

A **rebus** is a puzzle that uses pictures in place of words, or parts of words.

up above

the

like a

in the

_____

_____

Use the pictures to solve the puzzle. Then write your answers on the lines.

This space shuttle needs to get back to Earth. Can you show it how to get there?

What Comes Next?

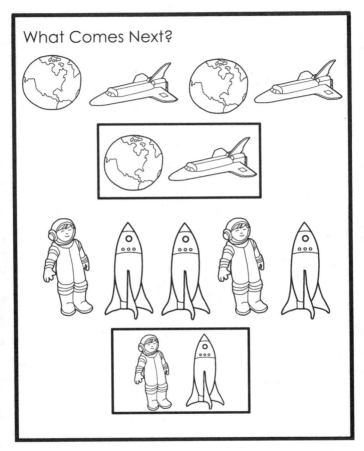

There is a pattern above each box. Circle the picture in the box that comes next in each pattern.

35

Look carefully at this picture of an astronaut.

Find and circle five things that make this picture different from the one opposite.

The moon is surrounded by twinkling stars. Count the stars, then circle the correct number.

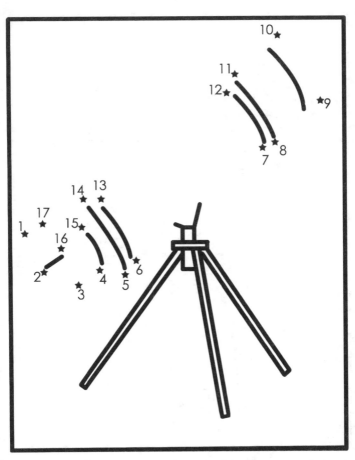

This object allows you to see the stars right from your window!
Connect the numbered stars to see what it is.

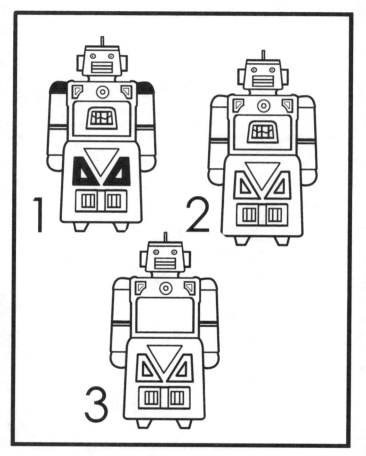

These six robots look the same, but only two are identical.

40

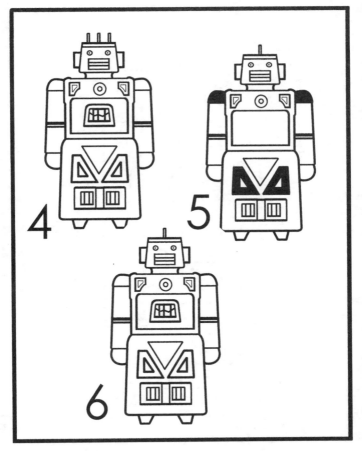

Find and circle the two that are the same.

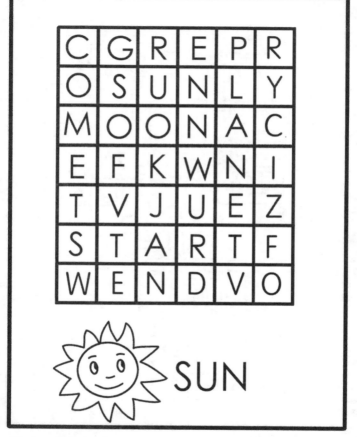

C	G	R	E	P	R
O	S	U	N	L	Y
M	O	O	N	A	C
E	F	K	W	N	I
T	V	J	U	E	Z
S	T	A	R	T	F
W	E	N	D	V	O

SUN

Find and circle the name of each picture clue in the puzzle.
The clues are on this page and the one opposite.

42

STAR

COMET

MOON

PLANET

Remember to look both across and down in the puzzle.

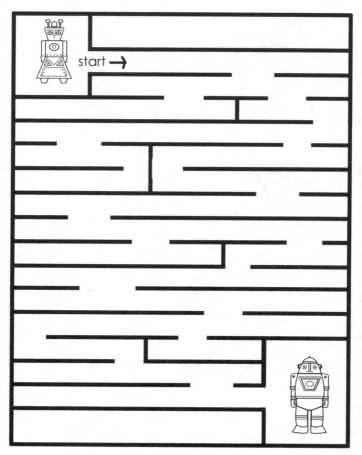

start →

This robot would like to get to her friend. Can you show her the right way to go?

44

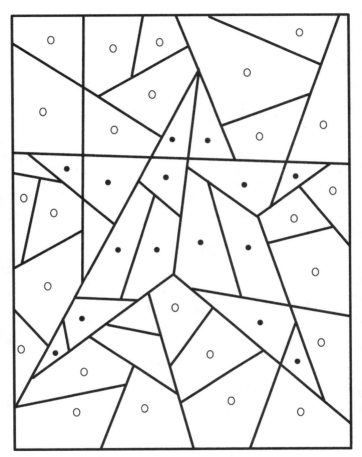

What shines brightly in a night sky? Color the spaces with a
• yellow and the spaces with a ○ blue to find out.

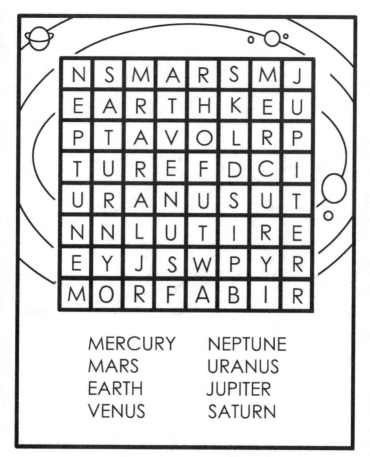

N	S	M	A	R	S	M	J
E	A	R	T	H	K	E	U
P	T	A	V	O	L	R	P
T	U	R	E	F	D	C	I
U	R	A	N	U	S	U	T
N	N	L	U	T	I	R	E
E	Y	J	S	W	P	Y	R
M	O	R	F	A	B	I	R

MERCURY   NEPTUNE
MARS   URANUS
EARTH   JUPITER
VENUS   SATURN

Find and circle the names of all eight planets in the puzzle.
Remember to look both across and down.

46

These five spaceships look the same, but only two are identical.
Find and circle the two that are the same.

47

The letters **P, L, A, N, E,** and **T** are hidden in the outer space scene above. Color in each letter.

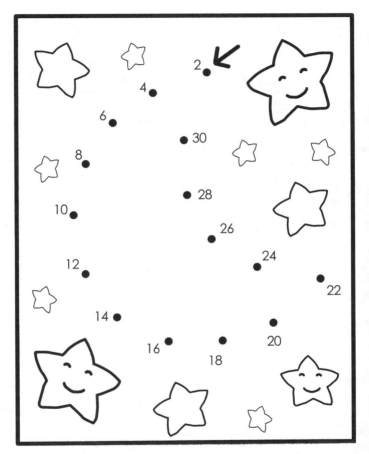

Here is something you can see only at night. Count by twos to connect the dots and find out what it is. Start at the arrow.

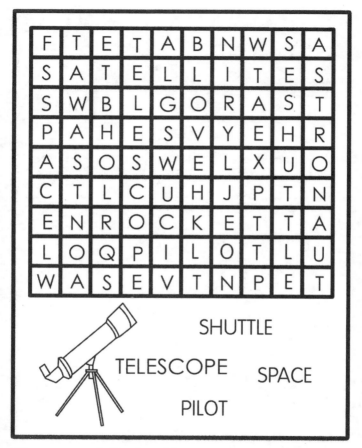

F	T	E	T	A	B	N	W	S	A
S	A	T	E	L	L	I	T	E	S
S	W	B	L	G	O	R	A	S	T
P	A	H	E	S	V	Y	E	H	R
A	S	O	S	W	E	L	X	U	O
C	T	L	C	U	H	J	P	T	N
E	N	R	O	C	K	E	T	T	A
L	O	Q	P	I	L	O	T	L	U
W	A	S	E	V	T	N	P	E	T

SHUTTLE

TELESCOPE   SPACE

PILOT

The seven words listed on this page and the one opposite are hidden in the puzzle.

50

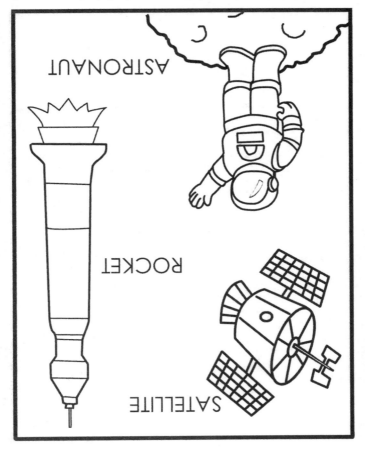

Find and circle each word. Be sure to look both across and down in the puzzle.

What Comes Next?

There is a pattern above each box. Circle the picture next in the box that comes next in each pattern.

Solutions

Page 4

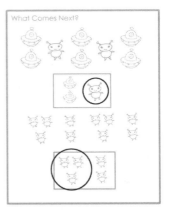

Page 6

Page 9

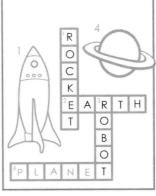

Page 10

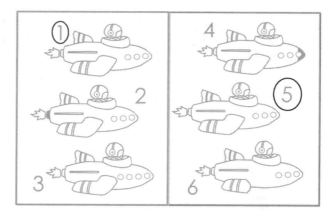

Pages 12–13

Page 14

Page 16

Page 18

Page 20

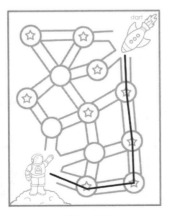

Page 21

Page 22

Page 23

Page 25

Page 27

Pages 28–29

Page 31

Pages 32–33

Page 34

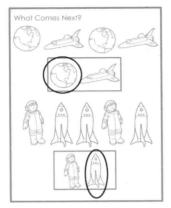

Page 35

Page 37

Page 38

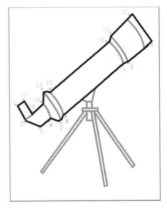

Page 39

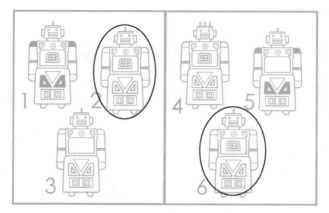

Pages 40–41

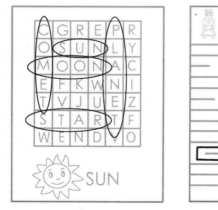

Page 42

Page 44

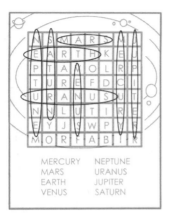

Page 46

Page 47

Page 48

Page 49

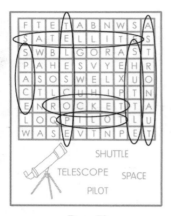

Page 50

Page 52

64